Giovanna Magi

W9-AXE-798

SALZBURG

Foreword by
Erich Landgrebe

93 COLOR ILLUSTRATIONS

BONECHI VERLAG STYRIA

Vertrieb
für Österreich
VERLAG STYRIA, A-8011 GRAZ,
Schönaugasse 64

für die Bundesrepublik Deutschland
LAHN VERLAG, Wiesbadener Straße 1
D-6250 Limburg/Lahn

© Copyright 1989 by CASA EDITRICE BONECHI
Via Cairoli, 18b Firenze
Telex 571323 CEB
Telefax 576844

Printed in the E.E.C. by
Centro Stampa Editoriale Bonechi.

Photographs by
Luigi Di Giovine

Translated by
John Sweet

ISBN 88-7009-077-9

HISTORICAL OUTLINE

In prehistoric times the entire Saltzburg area was covered by the sea, and it is from this period that its wealth derives; salt became in fact the centre around which its future history would develop. Already in 300 B. C. the salt began to be extracted and today it is not yet exhausted. In 41 A. D., under the Emperor Claudius, Saltzburg, known as the Juvavia colony, became a municipal city. The germanic Erulians burned it to the ground around the year 500 and in the sixth century Rupert appeared who became patron of the city until the present day; St. Peter's was constructed and the city became the seat of a bishop, at a time when the main resources of the area were still based on the extraction of salt. In 754 Bishop Virgilius built the first Cathedral and in the 8th century there is the first documentary evidence of the city. The Scribes School was founded at Saltzburg, Charlemagne arrived, the archbishop received the right to mint coins; following all this the city fell prey to the struggle between the pope and the emperor. To whom did Saltzburg belong? This was a power game that lasted for a good eight centuries. To whom was its archbishop subject, to the temporal power or to the spiritual one?

The archbishop, whose diocese stretched from High Bavaria to Stiria, from Zittertal to Wiener Neustadt, is not in fact a cardinal, yet he has the right to wear the purple. As a prince regent he was completely subject to the emperor or the king, but owing to the salt, the copper and the gold from the Tuarus he was much richer than the other prince regents who were jealous of him. In this way the archbishops became ever more powerful and the city depended on them alone for its good and bad times. The citizens tried everything to defend their rights and founded the "Igelbund," according to which they would pay homage to the new prince only when he had redressed some of the abuses existent in the city. In reality however things were completely different: the moment the prince came to power the promises became worthless. Is it possible that the Saltzburg Festival in fact began in the year 1000: one arrived from outside, became famous and lived an extravagant existence...

Around 1500 a great man brought order to the city with a fist of iron: the archbishop Leonard von Keutschach, rough, aristocratic and without scruples, but generous, a contemporary of Dürer and Breughel, a man who stands betweem the Middle Ages and modern times. The money he minted was called "Rübentaler," that is turnip thalers (on his coat of arms there was a turnip), and he himself was nick-named the "Biersieder" (the brewer). The "Stier" (Bull) of the fortress, the famous organ, was originated by him. This instrument was intended to call the citizens of Salzburg to work and to rest. A curious anecdote is told of Keutschach about how he organised a sleigh ride for the councillors. The councillors had purposely chosen a mayor who, for his sympathy for the emperor, did not please Keutschach. Keutschach invited the councillors to a meeting where they were taken by surprise, put in chains and made to go up and down in sleighs, exposed to the intense January cold until they gave up their guanteed rights in writing.

The modern age arrived: Paracelsus, a doctor and alchemist, returned to Salzburg, he is one of the most important personalities of this age. The Reformation was felt in two peasants' revolts; the first printing press was founded here and in 1587 Wolf Dietrich von Raitenau was elected archbishop at the age of 28. It was this man who gave Saltzburg its true appearance. A man of the world, he went about the streets armed and only gave up his sword at the door of the church. New bridges, palaces, squares and roads were built and when the Cathedral caught fire it is reported that he said, "If its is burning, let it burn!" It is possible to believe that he himself was responsible for the fire for a new Cathedral was immediately planned and entire rows of houses were demolished to create more space. The Mirabell was built as the archbishop's palace and, as he was also a worldly prince, for his mistress Salome Art, by whom it is said, that he had ten or more children.

At the time of the "Salt War" Dietrich von Raitenau fled at the arrival of the Bavarian troops, he was captured however and was held prisoner in the fortress until his death, by his cousin and enemy, Marcus Sitticus, who succeeded him in the high office. In 1620

Paris Lodron was elected and governed for 34 years, that is for the entire duration of the Thirty Years War, but he was able to preserve the city from the disorders by his politics of neutrality. He drained the marshes surrounding the city, founded the university and celebrated for eight days and nights the consecration of the Cathedral. It was Lodron who brought to conclusion the great work of Wolf Dietrich and of the ploughman Leonard von Keutschach. Around 1700 the architect Bernard Fischer von Erlach was sent for, he built the harmonious Dreifaltigkeitskirche (the church of the Holy Trinity), the fantastic Kollegienkirche (College) and the moving Spitalkirche (the Hospice church) and the enormous castle of Klessheim. Thus the exhuberant Baroque motifs were placed alongside the Italians lines of the city. In 1756 a man named Leopold Mozart announced: "I wish to communicate that on the 27th January, at eight in the evening, my wife happily gave birth to a son. His name is Johannes Chrysostomomos Wolfgang Gottlieb."

In 1803 the archbishopric was secularized and became an electorate until 1805. It then came under the sovereignty of Austria and, four years later, it fell to the French, a year later still it was under the Bavarians, and finally in 1816 it became the subject capital of upper Austria, reduced to an obscure province, a town of 12,000 inhabitants. Today there are ten times as many. Saltzburg is not only "the beautiful city," as it was described by its great poet Georg Trakl, but it is also a very particular city in that it has never belonged to those to whom a city normally belongs, that is its citizens. Until the 18th century the city was the property of the archbishops. After an insignificant 19th century it belonged to foreigners and to the world. As always it leads a double life: it oscillated for centuries between ecclesiastical and regal sovereignity and nows it oscillates between being a provincial city and a city of the world, between a meeting place for the wide world and a meeting place of farmers, between the graceful Baroque and the Bavarian brewery at Mülln.

Erich Landgrebe

The Hohensaltzburg fortress seen from the river.

HOHENSALZBURG FORTRESS

From 542 metres high on the Mönchsberg the powerful fortress of Hohensalzburg has, for nine centuries, been the characteristic land-mark so important to the city of Saltzburg, and not only to the city but to the whole surrounding region, for its century-laden bulk is visible and recognizable for miles around.

This is, without doubt, the largest and best preserved of all the castles and fortress that have come down to us from the Middle Ages.

Long ago in 1077 Gebhard, the Archbishop of Saltzburg, commenced its construction. A year earlier the struggle for the investitures had begun which set the Emperor Henry IV on one side, against Pope Gregory VII on the other. Profitting from the absence of Henry IV in Italy Gebhard also took position and, during the election of the anti-king Rudolf of Swabia, he supported the German electors. Then, fearing that the Emperor on his return might be offended, he hurriedly fortified the summit that dominated the town of Werfen and the rock that stood over the old city of Salzburg. This was the original nucleus of the

present fortress and probably, as was the case with all similar buildings of the period, it was built at first of wood.

Enlargements and modifications began almost at once. The archbishop Konrad, 1106-1147, may be considered if not its founder, its real builder. The building, in Romanesque style, consists of a battlemented wall surrounding the inhabited tower.

It began to take on its present appearance however from the 15th century when an enlargement of the fortress was made necessary, partially due to the growing conflict with the emperor, and partially to the fear of Turkish invasion. In

5

The Hohensaltzburg Fortress – The Lodron Arch.

The Hohensaltzburg Fortress – The Reiszug.

The Hohensaltzburg Fortress – The court-yard.

The Hohensaltzburg Fortress – The granary.

fact, many years later (in 1529) the Turks would arrive at the walls of Vienna.

First Johann II von Reisberg constructed two ramparts, one to the south and the other to the east; then Archbishop Burchard von Weisspriach added four large, round towers, of which one is now lost; in 1479 Bernhard von Rohr lived in the fortress and was succeeded by Johannes II Beckenschlager. At this point it was refortified by the famous archbishop Leonard von Keutschach in Late Gothic style and he also rendered it inhabitable. To him are owed the Chapel of St. George, the stretch of wall that runs from the "Trumpeters Tower" to the "Horses Gate" (or Rossp-forte); so-called as it was possible to pass beneath it on horseback, and the Reiszug, also called "die Reise." The latter is a rack-rail, constructed by the powerful archbishop in 1504, which, for 304 metres, crosses the fortress from the Nonnberg a good five times. Many people contributed to the construction of the Reiszug: at first prisoners held in the castle and later animals (horses and oxen) supplied the labour.

For the prince-archbishops the fortress was not only a splendid residence but it was often and fortunately a heaven-sent refuge. Proof was given of this in 1525 when the peasants in revolt had taken the city and laid seige to the fortress. Only providential help from the Swabian League led by Ludwig of Bavaria and Georg von Frunsberg freed the archbishop locked within its aged walls.

Through the long centuries that passed the fortress was continually remodelled and strengthened (the work of Paris Lodron was very significant).

The fortress fell to the French in 1803 when Napoleon drew close and for a long time was left abandoned. Only in 1861 radical restoration was undertaken (most recently the fortress has been strengthened with injections of cement) and it was transformed: no longer a prison, no longer a treasury, no longer a barrack but simply a marvellous place, witness to the centuries of life in Salzburg, and open to the public.

The Hohensaltzburg Fortress – St. George's Chapel.

The Hohensaltzburg Fortress – The chaplain's house.

A visit to the Hohensalzburg fortress is one of the most interesting and picturesque that it is possible to make in Salzburg.

Either on foot, or by the curious rack-rail cable car, one goes up to the fortress until the first "defensive arch" is reached, this is none other than the Arch of Lodron, a powerful round suppressed arch on which is sculpted the arms of the archbishop who ordered its construction. And so, by means of arches and passage-ways, alongside towers and battlements, it is possible to reach the pretty court-yard shaded by lime trees, hundreds of years old. Here the granary of 1484 bears the double stem of the archbishop Johann, and the slender line of the church's bell-tower, ordered by Leonard von Keutschach in 1502 in honour of St. George, may be seen. Beyond a cistern of 1539 that conveyed the water from the roofs by a system of pipes, a splendid bass-relief in red Salzburg marble representing Archbishop Leonard in the act of benediction may be admired; he is flanked by two deacons, one who supports the Gospels and the other holds the archbishop's hat and cross. The sculptor Hans Valkenauer executed it in 1515 and it is one of the loveliest examples of Gothic style in the whole Salz-

The Hohensaltzburg Fortress –
The bass reliefs representing
Archbishop Leonard von Keutschach.

The Hohensaltzburg Fortress – The Saltzburger Stier.

The Hohensaltzburg Fortress – A room in the museum.
The Hohensaltzburg Fortress – The Goldene Stube.

burg region, higher up another bass-relief represents Christ on the Cross with the Madonna and St. John.

A visit of the rooms inside contains no fewer surprises: the first is the "Salzburger Stier," literally the "Bull of Salzburg": it is a cylindrical organ built in 1502, so-called because the initial and the final chord imitate the bellowing of a bull. Worked by hand it has a roll mechanism that plays classical tunes three times a day (at seven, at eleven and at six).

There is also a museum in the Hohensalzburg Fortress, the Castle Museum. It has been reorganized in the so-called "old State rooms," on the floor below the apartments of the prince-bishops. In these rooms there is a beautiful ceiling with wooden beams of the latter half of the 15th century, held up, where the area is very wide, by pillars standing in the centre of the room.

Among the various objects kept in the museum of particular interest are the models and designs for

The Hohensaltzburg Fortress – The Goldene Stube: a detail of the door.

The Hohensaltzburg Fortress – The Goldene Stube: the majolica stove.

The Hohensaltzburg Fortress – The ramparts.

The Hohensaltzburg Fortress – The rack-railway

the construction of the fortress, some instruments of torture, documents and exhibits of medieval art. However, the undisputed symbol of the ancient splendour of the fortress is seen by a visit to the apartments. The "Goldene Stube", or Room of Gold, offers a sight worthy of the name it bears. It is decorated with pictures and carved wood, with garlands and rosettes on the lacu- nar ceiling, and enhanced by a door decorated with stylized vine branches. The room is dominated by a maiolica stove that stands four metres high, it was made in 1501 and is truly a masterpiece of its kind: eight lions support its heavy mass which is covered in reliefs of saints, allegorical figures, flowers, heraldry and religious symbols.

The view of Saltzburg
from the Hohensaltzburg fortress

14

A view of the Cathedral.

Cathedral – The facade.

CATHEDRAL

Throughout its long and turbulent history three huge squares (the Residenzplatz, the Kapitelplatz and the Domplatz) have surrounded this very beautiful example of pure Baroque.

On the same site that the present Cathedral occupies today existed a primitive building that was consecrated by Virgil, an Irish bishop, in 774 where the bones of St. Rupert were deposited. This ancient edifice had a nave, two aisles and was 66 metres long. Frequently damaged by fires, it was completely destroyed by fire on the IIth December 1598. Archbishop Dietrich then ordered its definitive reconstruction and having destroyed everything that remained standing he employed the architect Vincenzo Scamozzi from Vicenza for this work. However, despite the fact that the foundations had already been laid, in 1611 the archbishop fell into disgrace and was removed. Three years later the Regent, Marcus Sitticus, ordered another great Italian, Santino Salari from Como, to bring the construction of the cathedral of Salzburg to its completion. In 1628 the church was solemnly consecrated by Paris Lodron. The façade is in a very pure and balanced Baroque style with slender towers, 82 metres high, which enclose the central body of the church and is decorated with statues of saints. Beneath the façade

Cathedral – A detail of the central portal, St. Martin sharing his cloak with the beggar, by Giacomo Manzù.

Cathedral – A detail of the right portal, Hope by E. Mataré.

are **three modern bronze portals** (1957-1958): the one on the right, by the German, E. Mataré, symbolises *Hope;* the one on the left is by the Austrian Schneider-Manzel and represents *Faith* with the miracle of Saul; the central door is by the Italian Giacomo Manzù and symbolises *Charity:* St. Martin giving his cloak to the beggar.

The sense of grandeur that we felt when we first drew near to the church does not leave us when we enter its interior: a huge nave and two aisles with transcepts and a dome over the crossing. It is very rich in works of art: paintings by the Italians Solari, Mascagni and Francesco di Siena, one of the most famous organs in Europe with 120 stops and ten thousand pipes; the most beautiful piece however is, without a doubt, *the baptisimal font,* signed by a "Meister Heinrich" in 1321: it is a bronze basin with bishops and abbots in relief supported by lions which form the base. The cover, by Schneider-Manzel, was made in 1958.

A stairway in the south transcept leads to the church's crypt which was restored in 1957-1959 and the tombs of the archbishops are located here. During the works foundations of the building of 1611 came to light.

Cathedral – A view of the interior.

Cathedral – The baptesimal font.

A night view of the Residenzbrunnen.

RESIDENZBRUNNEN

This stands in the middle of the Residenzplatz and is generally considered to be the most beautiful Baroque fountain on this side of the Alps. It is the Residenzbrunnen, a pyramidical work including horses, dolphins, atlantes and a triton. It was commissioned in 1660 by Archbishop Guidobald Thun, perhaps from Tommaso da Garona; it is likely that the author was influenced by Bernini's Triton fountain in Rome, particularly regarding the new conception of the fountain which now became an essential element in the lay out and architectural space of its setting. The fountain lives in all its fascination at night when all the lights around it are off.

RESIDENZ

The Residenzplatz: the largest and most lively square in the city is surrounded on all sides by imposing buildings. On the west side of the square stands the Residenz Palace, this grandiose building was constructed between 1595 and 1619 as the official residence of the prince-archbishops of Saltzburg and remained so until the year in which Napoleon arrived. It was enlarged by Lukas von Hildebrandt; one enters the palace through the court-yard of honour in which there is the eye-catching **Fountain of Hercules** of 1605, the water spurts from the mouths of stags carved along the side of the basin. During the summer operas are put on in the court-yard, mainly those of Mozart. The second floor of the Residenz consists of 15 chambers each more magnificently furnished than the next with tapestries, period furniture, stucchi, and paintings. Some are rich in history: in the *Concert Hall* the child Mozart performed together with his sister; the *Audience Chamber* is also called the Tapestry Chamber as the walls are hung with three large Gobelin tapestries, made in 1710, the same year that the room was furnished; the *Hall of the Carabinieri,* 50 metres long and 12 metres wide, was once used as the headquarters of the archbishop's body-guard: today, below the ceiling decorated by Michael Rottmayr in 1689, the regional government holds sumptous public receptions and has done so since it took possession of the building after the abdication of Colloredo in 1803. This is the largest of the Residenz's chambers. It was built around 1600 and was heightened 65 years later. It was inaugurated on the 27th January 1614 when the operatic cycle of the "Telaribühne" was performed. Still today when performances cannot take place in the open due to bad weather, the stage is set up in this chamber, at the far end where there is a lovely double stairway in marble with balustrade.

The rich collection of the works of art hung in the 14 rooms of the third floor of the palace was ob-

The façade of the Residenz, seen from above.

Residenz – The court-yard.

Residenz – The Hercules Fountain.

Residenz – The Concert Chamber.
Residenz – The Audience Chamber.

Residenz – The Hall of the Carabinieri.

Residenzgalerie – A room.

The Residenzbrunnen and the Glockenspiel.

tained by the regional government at the same time: the **Residenz-galerie** also includes the central nucleus of the famous Viennese Czernin collection, which was bought by the city of Salzburg in 1955. The Italians are represented there with paintings by Guercino, Tiepolo, Barocci; the Flemish and the Dutch by Van Cleve, Rembrandt, Vermeer, Rubens; the French by Le Sueur and Poussain and the Austrians by Maulpertsch, Rottmayr up to Gustav Klimt.

GLOCKENSPIEL

Opposite the Residenz is the Neu Residenz, constructed at the end of the 16th century by Archbishop Wolf Dietrich for the prince-arch-bishops while the reconstruction work on the Residenz rendered it temporarily uninhaitable. When the archbishop returned to his usual seat the new building was used for the numerous and frequent guests of the prince in Saltzburg.

The tower called the Glockenspiel is a part of the palace, this name derives from the Dutch carillon that Archbishop Johann Ernst bought in 1695 for 1000 gold ducats from the famous caster Melchior de Haze, in Antwerp. Its 35 bells were cast in 1702 and inaugurated three years later. Since then the carillon has played regularly, three times a day. Still today, just as when it was new, a dense crowd gathers in the square to hear its characteristic and melodious sound.

MOZARTPLATZ

It is impossible that Salzburg's great genius should not have a square in his city; the statue is not a great masterpiece, it is neither more nor less than a dutiful homage to a great citizen. It was erected in 1842 from a design by Ludwig von Schwanthaler and unveiled in the presence of the musician's children. Such simplicity however is deceptive: it is difficult to find, anywhere in the world, a city that loves its famous son as Salzburg loves Mozart.

A curiousity: while the excavations were being made to lay the foundations of the monument Roman remains came to light, amongst which was a fragment of a mosaic floor which bore the Latin inscription "Hic habitat Felicitas." What lovelier homage to a city?

The houses that line the sides of the square often hide unsuspected treasures: number 4, for example, has a small court-yard, in its peace and quiet its almost a cloister, closed on the far side by a graceful chapel of about 1770.

Nearby is the **House of George Trakl,** the poet. Born in 1887 he died in Cracovia, aged 27, from

Mozartplatz and the statue to Mozart. **Mozartplatz, no. 4.**

an overdose of drugs; he was driven to this madness by the horrors of the First World War. Of his brief creative period remain poetical works of extraordinary power, these include *Gedichte* (1913), *Sebastian im Traum* (posthumous, 1915), and *Der Herbst Einsamen* (posthumous, 1920). His poems reflects sadness, melancholy and a feeling of guilt. The images that Trakl created with his imagination, at times difficult to understand, exercise an overhelming fascination upon men of our own time.

ALTER MARKT

As a result of the expansion of the city between the 11th and the 14th century the old market was transferred here from the Waagplatz where it was originally situated.

Today, now that the square is closed to traffic and reserved only for pedestrians, its beauty and all its characteristics may be enjoyed to the full: from *the statue of St. Florian,* of 1734 with beautiful renaissance railings, *to the ex-Court Pharmacy,* with valuable vases from the 17th and 18th centuries; from the smallest house of the city, to the very pleasant *Tomaselli Café,* founded by an Italian in 1703.

GETREIDEGASSE

The Getreidegasse is the oldest of the city's streets, it is also the most chaotic, the most lively, the most picturesque: there is proof that in the 12th century it was already called Trabgasse, or Tragasse, from the word "trabig" which means "alive," "animated."

The houses that line the street are high, narrow and richly decorated, embellished with signs in wrought iron and wood with lively paintings that illustrate the business of the different shops on which they are hung.

Altermarkt.

Getreidegasse.

Getreidegasse – A typical court-yard.

MOZART'S BIRTHPLACE

It is almost impossible to speak of Salzburg and not mention Mozart, not only because the musician was born here and lived here for most of his life, but also because everything in Salzburg is so permeated with musicality and harmony that the fact that one of mankind's greatest geniuses was born here seems almost natural. He was born in the house at number 9 Getreidegasse: the owner was Hagenauer, a shop-keeper, who had bought it in 1713 from Chunrad Froeschlmoser, the Court chemist. In November 1747 the Mozart family, consisting of Leopold Mozart, his wife Anna Maria Pertl and their six children, moved into the third floor of the building: the seventh child, Wolfgang Amadeus, was born on the 27th January 1756. The father, a musician, immediately directed him to the study of the harpsicord and Mozart very quickly showed himself to be a true "enfant terrible." His very first studies in composition date from 1759 and in 1762 he wrote his first minuet and the *Allegro in B flat*. And here they are, the first studies by Mozart written in the exercise book of his sister Nannerl; the piano was made in Vienna by Anton Walter with walnut hammers, a register of five octaves and knee pedals. Mozart played many of his concerts on this piano. How many? Mozart's musical production is truly remarkable, particularly if one considers that he died young in 1791. The compositions contained in the 1862 catalogue (each preceded, as is known, by the letter K), a good 626 in number, including 21 operas, 49 symphonies, 5 concertoes for violin and orchestra, 35 sonatas for violin and piano 25 concertoes for piano and orchestra and 23 string quartets.

Mozart's birthplace – The façade.

Mozart's birthplace – A portrait of Mozart by Joseph Lange.

Mozart's birthplace The musicians piano

THE CAROLINO-AUGUSTEUM MUSEUM

This museum is dedicated to the history and art not only of Saltzburg but also of the region and is therefore very interesting and worth a short visit.
It is arranged according to the most modern ideas of museography and covers a wide and complete range of interests: from early evid-

Carolino-Augusteum Museum – The entrance hall.

Carolino-Augusteum Museum – Beak-jug.

Carolino-Augusteum Museum – Altar-piece, the Adoration of the Magi, by the Master of the Virgo inter Virgines.

Altes Burgerspital.

ence of the pre-historic age, such as the bronze age *helmet,* to archeological finds of the celtic age, such as the exquisitely shaped *beak vase* found in 1932 on the Dürrnberg at Hallein, it is dated about 350 B.C. and is made of a single piece of bronze; in it Celtic, Etruscan and Scythian styles are recognizable, all fused together; from pictures of the 15th century to the finest examples of Gothic painting, such as the *Two Saints* by Konrad Leib or the *reredos of the Adoration of the Magi* by the Master of the Virgo inter Virgines.

ALTES BURGERSPITAL

This building, which houses the civil hospital, was already operating for the aged of the city in 1327. It is set back, almost squashed against the face of the Mönchsberg. The main building was reconstructed between 1556 and 1562 and still today one is struck by the boldness with which such an imposing building is inserted into such a limited space, not suffocated by the cliff face that stands above it, but so in harmony with it that it almost completes it.

This side of the building seems to us unusually harmonious and elegant due to the heavy, sculpted corbels that support the arcade of the ground floor and to the two upper rows of round arches on red, marble pillars.

Behind the arcades, carved into the rock, are the cells called *Pfrundnerzellen* and the cellars.

The upper part of the building, in which there are eye-like round windows, was added in 1570.

SIGMUNDPLATZ

If we are in the Sigmundplatz then we are in one of the most characteristic places of the old city, particularly by night when the magical play of light on the Pferdeschwemme can be enjoyed. This is a drinking trough for horses that was constructed in 1695 to cover a stone quarry. The design of the complicated and unusual monument is by the great Fischer von Erlach the Elder, while the sculptural group of the horse tamed by man is by B. M. Mandl. The horse may be said to be the protagonist of this monument and in fact is again represented in the lively paintings and frescoes on the walls.

The Pferdeschwemme.

The Pferdeschwemme and the Festspielhaus.

Festspielhaus.

FESTSPIELHAUS

The huge building, for which in 1693 Fischer von Erlach designed the lovely Baroque façade that faces the Sigmundplatz, was occupied by the old riding school. Its conversion was begun in recent times when two theatres were made on the site of the summer riding-ground. Later on, in 1960, when the crowds of spectators were so great that there was not enough space it was decided to build another theatre capable of holding more than two thousand people.

The originator of this project was the Austrian, Clemens Holzmeister, who carved out a good one hundred thousand cubic metres of rock from the overhanging hill, to obtain the space for the stage. Today the acoustics of the theatre are perfect: famous modern artists such as Oscar Kokoschka wanted to make their contribution to this splendid achievement of man's genius and decorated the auditorium with their bold and very colourful works.

REINHARDT PLATZ

The square beside the Kollegien-kirche is the Reinhardt Platz, it is embellished by a fountain that was built in 1610 and was originally intended for the present Hanusch-platz. It is in the form of a basin on three levels and is completely surrounded by wrought iron railings with vine leaf decorations. In the centre a column supports a "wilder Mann" or "Tattermann," who carries the coat of arms of the city of Salzburg.

KOLLEGIENKIRCHE

When the Austrian Baroque freed itself from Italian influence and took on an increasingly personal form, then the church of the ancient University was built from designs by Fischer von Erlach the Elder. It was constructed alongside the University at the beginning of the 17th century.

Begun in 1696, it was consecrated in 1707: the exterior has a façade whose square side towers enclose the convex central body; the inte-rior is on a central plan with side chapels and is covered by an enor-mous dome with stucco work by D. F. Carlone.

The four side chapels are dedicated to the faculties of theology, medi-cine, law and philosophy and to their patrons, St. Thomas Aquinas St. Luke, St. Ivo, and St. Benedict respectively.

The other arts and sciences are also portrayed in the different sym-bolic representations in the church: Music, Painting, Philosophy, Juris-prudence and Medicine are all re-presented by means of allegorical statues that decorate the high altar.

Reinhardtplatz – The fountain with the « Tatterman ».

Kollegienkirche.

FRANZISKANER-KIRCHE

Few churches are able to evoke in the visitor such an immediate response as the Franciscan church in Saltzburg. Its fame, its beauty and its distinctiveness derive from the contrast between the three styles — Romanesque, Gothic and Baroque — that meet and mingle harmoniously in the interior.

In fact from the gloomy, dim light of the typically Romanesque nave and aisles of the crossing one suddenly passes into the blinding brightness of the Gothic choir and chancel with a nave and two aisles, the work of Hans von Burghausen; and from its splendid pureness of line, from its very pure star vaulting supported by a single, very slender, central pillar, one passes into the rich Baroque of the altars in the 17th century side chapels. In this magnificent interior therefore there is a very subtle intellectual play of line and of colour; moreover it encloses two very lovely artistic masterpieces: the *pulpit*, in the most typical Romanesque style, with a lion motif supporting the column; and on the high altar by Fischer von Erlach, a sculpted Gothic *Madonna* in lime wood by Michael Pacher. The seated statue of the Virgin is all that remains of a triptych commissioned by the city of Saltzburg in 1484 from the great sculptor. Pacher worked here from 1486 to 1498 for a salary of 3500 Rhenish florins. The altar was dismantelled in 1709; neither is the figure of the Child original, it was made in 1890 by J. Piger, a sculptor from Saltzburg.

Franziskanerkirche – Madonna by Michael Pacher.

Franziskanerkirche – A detail of one of the lions that support the pulpit.

Franzkanerkirche – A view of the High Altar.

The Church of St. Peter – The exterior and the nave.

Peters-Friehof – An outside view of the cemetery.
Peters-Friehof – The chapel of St. Maximus.

ST. PETER

The Benedictine monastery was founded about 690, by the French bishop Rupert; a part of this church is the oldest in the whole of Salzburg.

The abbey, similar to many others, achieved great importance in the Middle Ages, concentrating in and calling to itself many geniuses, preaching the new ways of life and making valuable contributions to the history of art and culture; as, for example, manuscript illumination, typical of the Salzburg school.

As seen today the church has a very long body culminating in a Baroque tower. When the church was destroyed in 1127 by fire, it was rebuilt between 1130 and 1143 deriving obvious inspiration from the Saxon architecture at Hildesheim, seen in the alternation of pillar and column. What was left of the Romanesque was altered during the Baroque, from 1757 to 1780: the early lacunar ceiling was heightened on several occasions and altered into a vaulted ceiling. The interior, with a nave, two aisles and transcepts, is very bright due to the delicate blue of the Rococco stucchi that covers the whole of the architectural structure of the church with its rhythmical games. The original side aisle of the Romanesque church constitutes the left aisle while in the right aisle the chapels, in chronological succession, seem to condense and sum up in themselves the long centuries of the abbey's history.

The interior contains many tombs: beyond that of Michael Haydn, brother of the more famous Joseph, a musician also, is the 5th century *cenotaph of St. Rupert,* it bears a curious inscription from 1444 that reads thus: "When my light is spent, this city will be destroyed." It is almost superfluous to add in jest that the sarcofagus is always illuminated.

The church's masterpiece however is the *red marble tomb of Hans von Raitenau,* a colonel in the German army married to a very Florentine Medici, and killed during the struggle against the Turks: enclosed in armour the soldier bears a white cloth on his fore-head which refers to the wound he received.

Outside, alongside the church, is the picturesque **Peters-Friehof** the oldest cemetery of the city and still in use. It was laid out with colonnades in 1627. Beneath the arches, enclosed behind wrought iron railings, in which the local craftsmen

have shown their skill, are the tombs of the oldest families of Salzburg. There is the tomb of the Hagenauer family, the owners of the Mozarts' house; there is also the tomb of Santino Solari who ended his ardent life as architect and sculptor here in Salzburg; there is also the tomb of Mozart's sister Nannerl.

From here a narrow underground passage leads to the Mönschsberg caves, also known as the Salzburg catacombs. According to tradition this was already a place of Christian prayer and worship at the end of the Roman period but it has never been shown with certainty that burial ever took place here. Beyond the chapel of St. Gertrude is the **chapel of St. Maximus** in which, according to legend, the saint was killed together with 50 of his followers.

KAPITELSCHWEMME

In the huge open space of Kapitelplatz, directly in front of the Archbishop's palace, stands a beautiful fountain called the Kapitelschwemme. It is an old drinking trough for horses turned into a Baroque fountain from plans by J. A. Pfaffinger and which the sculptor Donner embellished, in 1732, with a group of *Triton* driven by Neptune.

NONNBERG CONVENT

The convent of the Benedictine nuns is situated on the eastern spur of the Mönchsberg. It also was founded by St. Rupert around the year 700: the first prioress, St. Erentrude, was his niece.

It is believed that this was actually the site of the "Salt Castle," the

Nonnberg Convent –
The fresco of St. Gregory.

Nonnberg Convent – Portal.

Kapitelschwemme.

first Saltzburg, from which the trade of this valuable mineral was supervised and controlled.

The church is of a much later date than the convent of which it is a part: it was in fact begun in Gothic style in 1463 and the Romanesque walls of the preceding building which had almost been completely destroyed by fire in 1423, were used in its construction.

It has a nave, two aisles and a choir with pretty Gothic *stained-glass windows* atributed to the school of Hans Wild da Ulm, and also a late Gothic *altar* carved by the famous Veit Stoss. The cript with its seven naves and 18 pillars that support the ribbed vault is also very picturesque. Here are the tombs of St. Erentrude and her sister in Christ, St. Regintrude.

The Nonnberg convent is also famous for its frescoes: the figure of St. Gregory is typical of a style and of an age. The saints are all represented in half figures, in rigidly frontal positions, with the facial features delineated to underline a deep spirituality and a solemn gravity.

ERHARDKIRCHE

The Nonntal area, situated on the spur of the Mönchsberg, offers the visitor glimpses of unexpected beauty and interesting monuments. This church dedicated to St. Erhard, was ordered by the Cathedral Chapter who entrusted its construction, between 1685 and 1689, to the Italian Gaspare Zugalli, an architect from Rovereto. To the sides of the church are the two hospice buildings for the attendants of the Chapter, one wing reserved for the men and one for the women. The church is in Baroque style: it is on a central plan with a majestic portico with four Ionic columns and a raised pediment (at one time the floods of the Nonntal were quite frequent in this area) set into the façade. The motif of the pediment is repeated in the two side towers that flank the elegant dome. The pretty double flight of stairs ably solves the problem of the lack of space and simultaneously gives movement to the whole of the front of the church.

Inside highly refined stucchi, both in relief and in the round, together with paintings by Altomonte and Rottmayr add to the church's value.

Erhardkirche – The façade.

The Papageno Fountain.

THE PAPAGENO FOUNTAIN

The bombs of the Second World War spared few areas of Saltzburg. But with the end of the fighting repair, reconstruction and embellishment was begun.

The opportunity was taken, therefore, during the work of reconstruction, to create a small square in which the citizens had a fountain built surmounted by a *statue of Papageno,* the bird-seller from the "Magic Flute" who, together with Prince Tamino, enters the kingdom of Sarastro to free the princess Pamina. He is one of the most delightful characters of the fable by E. Schikaneder, which Mozart set to music in 1791.

Sebastianskirche – The exterior.

Sebastianskirche – The tomb of Paracelsus.

The panorama of the Kapuzinerberg with the Hettwer ramparts and the monastery.

KAPUZINER-KLOSTER

The Kapuzinerberg, a mass of dolomitic rock and lime-stone, rising on the bank of the Salzach River, is the other hill that dominates the city. In historic times this hill was called the Imberg, as is shown by documents from 1319 and, in fact, the little church that was built here was called St. John on the Imberg. Tracts of the medieval circuit of walls and towers still stand out on the woodcovered slopes of the hill. It is still possible to appreciate the fortifications, directly below the monastery, which, since 1924, have been called *Hettwer's Ramparts*. Colonel Emil Hettwer earned a special respect from the people of Salzburg for his interest in works of art and his tireless efforts for the continual beautifying of the city. The Kapusinerkloster stands above it on the extreme western slope: the church dates from 1602 but the Gothic doors from an earlier building of 1450 still remain.

SEBASTIANSKIRCHE

The Sebastianskirche was rebuilt in Baroque style between 1749 and 1753, and is noted above all for the tombs of the famous people that it contains.

The first of these is Dr. *Theophrastus Paracelsus,* or rather, as the naturalist doctor Philipp Theophrast von Hohenheim loved to call himself, Philippus Aureolus Theophrastus Bombastus Paracelsus, taking the latin form! The son of a doctor,

having studied and graduated at Ferrara in Italy, he began to travel and to study the diseases most frequently contracted by the population, launching new theories that often and willingly brought him serious enmity and stirred up bitter arguments from those who, unlike himself, were more closely tied to tradition. It was thus that after he had been nominated professor at the University of Basle, he was forced to abandon his post and the city, and began again to wander through the various European countries that offered him asylum. Amongst these was Saltzburg where he died in 1541, the same year as his arrival.

His tomb, near to the entrance, is in Baroque style and contains the bones of the doctor and philosopher. The other great men are found in the **cemetery of St. Sebastian,** built by Andrea Bertoletto and which was, in 1600, Saltzburg's main cemetery. Surrounded by many arched chapels, it holds about a hundred tombs. Here several members of Mozart' family lie at rest: his father Leopold, who died in 1787, a daughter of his sister Nannerl, who died in 1805 and the musician's widow Costanza with her second husband Nikolaus von Nissen, advisor to the State of Denmark. The tomb of the greatest of the Mozart's, Wolfang, is missing; he died at Vienna and was buried in a common grave, no trace has ever been found of his body.

In the centre of the cemetery is the **Gabrielskapelle,** the mausoleum of Archbishop Wolf Dietrich, who died in 1603. It was built in a very pure Renaissance style by the architect Elia Castello: the interior is decorated with stucchi and mosaics and is dominated by a large dome covered with multi-coloured ceramic tiles.

The cemetery of St. Sebastian –
The Mozart family tomb.

The cemetery of St. Sebastian –
The interior of the Gabrielskapelle.

Dreifaltigkeitskirche.

DREIFALTIGKEITS-KIRCHE

The far end of the Makartplatz, which is named after the Saltzburg painter Hans Makart, is picturesquely occupied by the Church of the Trinity.

Its construction begun in 1694 by Fischer von Erlach the Elder and in style it resembles the Karlskirche in Vienna, the other church by the same architect which must be considered his masterpiece.

Here also, the main body of the church is enlivened by the continual undulation of the façade and is dominated by a dome which was originally much more overpowering, as the side towers were lower than at present: they were raised in fact in 1759 and again altered in 1818. In 1699 the sculptor Mandl decorated the façade with four statues representing Faith, Love, Hope and Wisdom.

51

THE MIRABELL CASTLE

When the castle was first erected in 1606 for Archbishop Wolf Dietrich it was not named Mirabell but Altenau; it received its present name from Dietrich's successor Archbishop Marcus Sitticus. **The Mirabell Gardens** are a marvellous and worthy introduction to the palace and in their planning and organization they carry the signature of Fischer von Erlach.

A fountain occupies the central part of the gardens; it is surrounded by four groups of statues that symbolize the four elements of the universe (air, water, earth and fire): they are the work of an Italian Ottavio Mosto who was born in Padua but lived in Salzburg where he carried out these works in 1690. A copper *Pegasus,* made in 1661 by Kaspar Gras, a sculptor from Innsbruck, was placed in front of the castle after 1913. These are not the only statues that enliven the Mirabell gardens, there are others which are very curious. A short distance from the Pegasus statue several marble dwarfs suddenly pop out of the greenery (this part of the garden is in fact popularly known as the garden of the little dwarfs); the statues were originally collected together in the "Zwergltheater" (or the Theatre of the Dwarfs) which was started by the Prince Archbishop Franz Anton Harrach and stood on the site of the present-day Schwarzstrasse, it was closed in 1811. The whole complex, the palace and the garden, was used as the summer residence of the prince-archbishops of Salzburg. The early building was enlarged between 1721 and 1727 by Lukas von Hildebrandt, who gave it a Baroque appearance: it was destroyed by a fire and received its present form due to alterations by Pietro de Nobile. In the interior, which is used by the local govern-

Mirabell – The castle
and the Italian Garden.

Mirabell – The statue of Pegasus.
Mirabell – One of the garden's dwarfs.

ment and the burghermeister, it is worth seeing the famous "Engels-stiege" or *Stairs of the angels,* an imposing marble stairway that leads to the first floor, the work of Raphael Donner. The statues of the cherubs and the putti that play along the balustrade are the best proof that the Austrian Baroque lived its finest moments here.

The stairs lead us to the *Marmorsaal,* whose walls are encrusted with marble and with gold stucchi: as it is now used for the celebration of civil marriage it is usually considered the "most beautiful registery office in Europe."

All this does nothing to increase Saltzburg's fame: here truly everythis is beautiful and also to get married takes on another meaning.

A detail of the « Angel's stairway ».

The Mirabell Castle – The Marmorsaal.

PARSCHKIRCHE

During the years 1955-1956 a group
of architects and engineers from
Saltzburg who called themselves
"Group 4" (Wilhelm Holzbauer,
Johann Spalt and Friedrich Kurrent
were all members) decided to con-
vert the stables of the last country
house that still existed in the Weich-
selbaum quarter into a church, the
first church of a modern design in
Saltzburg. In its simplicity and ab-
solute lack of decoration on the
exterior only three crosses show
that this is a church. The unusual
and very individual bell-tower lights
the interior which consists of a
huge hall in which the vaulting is
very low and of a choir on a higher
level. Oskar Kokoschka, Jakob Adl-
hart and Josef Mikl all contributed
to the decoration of the church.
The *Crucifix* over the north entrance of the church is by Fritz
Wotruba who was born in Vienna
in 1907. Here also this sculptor

Parschkirche – A view of the interior.
Parschkirche – Crucifix by F. Wotruba.

tackles a theme that has always been very dear to him, that of the human body conceived as an architectural structure, his favourite material is stone and his style is always suspended on the border between abstract and representative.

LEOPOLDSKRONE CASTLE

In 1727 Archbishop Leopold Anton Firmian decided to build this castle as a gift for his nephew Laktanz Firmian.

The architect Bernhard Stuart designed a three storied building crowned by a mansard and concluded with an octagonal tower which was transformed into Baroque style at the end of the 18th century.

Until 1828 the castle remained the property of the counts Firmian: it then changed hands repeatedly until 1918 when it was bought by Max Reinhardt, the famous German director (whose real name was Max Goldmann) who died in New York in 1943. He was director of the Deutsches Theater in 1905 and is considered to have reformed modern German theatre. He arranged it so luxuriously that he brought back to it the ancient splendour that it had once known but had lost with the passing of time.

KLESSHEIM CASTLE

Today a luxury hotel occupies this castle that was commissioned by Archbishop Johann Ernst, Count of Thun, in 1700 and which was entrusted to the skill of Fischer von Erlach. The palace was finished in 1709 but was only ready for occupation in 1732 when Leopold Anton Firmian was archbishop of Saltzburg. The coat of arms of two beautiful recumbent deer which stands at the foot of the ramp that leads up to the central building belongs in fact to this family. The central part of the building, opened by a large arcade, stands out against the side wings.

CHURCH OF MARIA PLAIN

The church was built from a design by G. A. Dario in 1671 to house a miraculous picture of the Virgin. On the 4th of July 1751 (which was the fifth saturday after Pentecost) a solemn ceremony was held in the church when the picture was placed on the high altar, having been enriched with a crown and a "rocaille" of silver. It is presumed that on the 28th anniversary of the event Mozart composed the famous "Krönungsmesse" or Coronation Mass that appears in the catalogue as composition K.V. 317.

The Leopoldskrone Castle.

The Klessheim Castle.

The church of Maria Plain.

Church of Maria Plain – Interior: the statue of the Virgin.

HELLBRUNN CASTLE

The first known settlements on the Hellbrunnerberg go back to prehistory; in the 15th century the whole of this huge area of royal property became an animal park. In 1613 Archbishop Marcus Sitticus employed Santino Solari to build a summer residence for him here. The castle was built in imitation of the Italian Baroque villas, particularly those around Rome and on the Venetian mainland, with jutting out wings, a square courtyard and the surroundig gardens. At Hellbrunn it was the latter however in which the fantasy, the caprice and the genius of its creators was let loose. During the first half of the 18th century, about 1730, the garden which had been laid out in Italian style was altered to French style.

Hellbrun Castle.

The main attraction of the garden that lies to the north and to the east of the castle are the fountains, the work of someone known only as Fra Gioacchino, who understood so well how to amuse the numerous guests of the archbishop.

In a small esedra, with statues in the niches, there is a stone table with some stone benches around it, by pressing a hidden mechanism the water spurts in small jets wetting and surprising the unsuspecting visitors.

From the gardens a road leads us to two of Hellbrunn's other curiosities: one is a small castle called *Monatsschlossl,* "the castle of a month," that is how long it took to build it: and certainly the archduke Maximilian, the grand duke of the Tyrol, must have been very surprised indeed when Archbishop Sitticus, whose guest he was, boasted to him of this uncommon undertaking.

The other curiosity is *the rock theatre* which was also constructed by Sitticus in 1613 and which made use of a natural cave that was converted into an open air theatre. Archbishop Sitticus, a great connoisseur and passionate patron of music and theatre, had Italian melodramas put on there.

Hellbrun Castle – The rock theatre.
Hellbrun Castle – The picturesque water effects.

ANIF CASTLE

FUSCHLSEE

Unfortunately neither the castle of Anif, nor its exceptional park, is open to the public, but even seen from afar its neo-Gothic architecture reflected in the water that surrounds it can make us realize how moving and picturesque this place is.

The castle is mentioned in documents of about 1550 and thereafter it fell completely into ruins until it was restored and radically changed by Count Arco-Stepperg between the years 1838 and 1848. The castle's court-yard contains a statue of a nymph, a small masterpiece carved in Carrara marble by Ludwig Schwanthaler about 1840.

On the far end of a tongue of land that juts out into the calm waters of lake Fuschl is the powerful but elegant mass of the castle of the same name; it was originally a hunting lodge for the prince-bishops of Saltzburg. It was restored during the 16th century and in the course of time has undergone a radical change, today it is a hotel in which famous people of the international world of politics and culture often and willingly meet. The castle's now distant origins are commemorated in the hunting museum which is arranged inside with typical exhibits of the art of hunting and a fine collection of weapons.

The Anif Castle.

The lake and the castle of Fuschl.

ST. GILGEN

Hardly twenty five kilometres from Saltzburg, laid out along the north bank of the Wolfgangsee, the town of St. Gilgen has the appearance of a pleasant holiday resort where peace and the beauty of the country side play the major parts.

The origin of the name is curious as there is no such saint. It probably derives from a popularization of St. Aegidius. In any case the village is very old. Traces of its existence date back to the year 830, when the lake that laps its shores was still called lake Aber as may be seen in several documents; the earliest construction of the parish church goes back to the 13th century.

St. Gilgen was the birthplace of Mozart's mother, Anna Maria Pertl, who was born here in 1720 her house still stands today (it is

St. Gilgen – The birthplace of Mozart's mother.

A view over the lake of St. Wolfga

The Church of St. Wolfgang – Interior: triptych by Michael Pacher.

the seat of the local government) and in front of it is a little statue of Mozart as a child playing a violin, a reminder that the musician often loved to spend time in his mother's home.

ST. WOLFGANG

In ancient times, when this place was still called Falkenstein, a bishop named Wolfgang lived a hermit's life here. It was the year 976 and many legends surrounded this holy man. It is also said that once, having climbed the highest rock, he threw an axe into the precipice, and he decided that there, where it landed, that a chapel should be built. Whatever the historical foundations of this legend may be the chapel of St. Wolfgang actually exists and contains a valuable treasure; the Gothic *triptych,* of 1481, the work of Michael Pacher.

It is necessary now to say a few words about this great sculptor, examples of whose wonderful work we have so often come across in Saltzburg.

Though he grew up in a Tyrolese environment (at any rate nordic by culture) he immediately accepted the influence of the "great studios" of Northern Italy, particularly that of Andrea Mantegna. The powerful sense of volume accompanied, above all in his wood carvings, with pictorial values created works with a high sense of drama, at the same time softened by tasteful colour.

INDEX